TWO FALL HAIKU

blow against my head
winds of autumn late morning
...let me feel freshly

your art deepens dark
the moon shines through your misting
silver everything

STORM HAIKU

there is a tempest
within the calm, a brewing
of the caldrom's sauce

everywhere i flee
i cannot stay i c annot
keep composure here

exceot the calm dies
and i sleep and dream beneath
these maniac winds

RACHEL HAIKU

sweetest little bird
acre of my longing heart
i live for you now

deep within my dreams
i sleep and think about you
meaning of my liife

i will always love
the treasure of our days here
love until i pass

FEAR HAIKU

i am so frightened
by everything strange, unlike
i used to feel things

i wake up with fear
and an ulicer against me
deep in my stomach

the days warm too much
the planet threatens us all
with an end to things

SMOKE HAIKU

you cannot breath it
speed of our hacking nostrls
cigarettes...carbon

co2 kills us
a weight against our sweating
a sterile poison

eat plants...they like it
they grow and root and blosson
and exhale pure air

MINDLESS HAIKU

dull thoughts through evening
lying uder greying skies
wander into dreams

mindless save for you
i lie awake and listen
to birds chattering

the pleasure of poetry
is the secret of your art

hidden in a face

MENTAL LIMITS HAIKU

after we first crack
there is the shivering at day
and slleepless nighttimes

we wander the words
the abyss of emotion
struggle a poem

the mind has limits
then its fail and falls apart
and we watch cell walls

WITCHCRAFT HAIKU

scissors lying flat
my grandma left them open
and died that way too

wickedly we watch
the world siink for greediness
while the world gets hot

love becomes tv
eat popcorn for our passion
wonder who we are

ENGLISHMAN HAIKU

the terrible hand
of a slave cut to strangle
a civilized mind

such broken ghosts call
years later....with vengeance come
to the white conscience

we all belong here
with god and nature binding
our equality

BRAIN FEVER HAIKU

not burning but itch

the fever i feel waking
from an achiness

all day i sit up
with a gastric pain throbbing
gnawing at my core

terrible fever
from fratures unhealed herein
stealing all my thoughts

PAIN HAIKU

when i try to sleep
i cramp and hurt all over

the pain is intense

asprin helps me dream
that numbing thinning pill dose
quietly in asleep

miracle drug works

slips me into sacred bliss
waiting for morning

FRACTURE HAIKU

split ribs at the core
terror upon the spinal
end of wind passing

pain in sharo relief
to the sky all blue and grey
above our head now

i feel like dying
at night when i cannot sleep
until i black out

REST HAIKU

lie down and snore up
the day is full of sunlight
and snoozes at noon

body aches from hurt
its damage is internal

slill sleep is helpfull

i disappear at day
am an echo of myself
sometimes at midday

THE CHILL THAT FOLLOWS HAIKU

the terrible cold bone ache
after a fracture opens
the side within us

days in the clinic
trying hard to sleep again
after a hard fall

shivering alone

away in the hospital
waiting for sleeping

DULL NIGHTS HAIKU

sleeplessness twisting
on a bed of thistles here
where the dark comes on

then during the day
a blinding light encircles
dark glasses against

night brings terrible
pain again we pray for dope
to keep out the pain

CRAWLING HAIKU

the southern swamp chills
toward a heartland of autumn
on the tiring hills

the moon tears as well
to raindrops full of twilight
in out dreadfull song

long ago we weot
now we break the weeping spell
that hooting owls kept

TELL YOU HAIKU

i wish i could speak
of the tenderness wiithin
tears of love i feel

with global warming
and all, the days still get cold
during november

i shiver while snows
melt away from the arctic
it is your coldness

FAT HAIKU

my girth surroounds me
full of undulating fat
tired elephant size

i breathe short breaths now
because of the weight of me
suffocating me

the pounds melt away
too tired to sustain themselves
too tired to stand up

ANXIOUS PAIN HAIKU

shivers of crystal
ice in the field of our cough
tossing and turning

the more we cough up
the worse we feel our aching
day and day asleep

imagine forests
full of lush vedgetation
to inhale and dream

SEDINTARY HAIKU

loafing on the porch
filling up the air we breath
the dust of autumn

silly cars drive by
on the distant avenue
in time...rain drops fall

i love and crave you
heart of mine, with a glazed look
think that way for you

AUTUMN NERVE HAIKU

i fall into hell
in the middle of autumn
and waste away now

dreaming nigbtmares each
day i am awake to this
horror of chilling

FALL ANXIETY HAIKU

i worry this fall
for seasons that don't come here
a colder journey

a colder place here
or sickly warm climate change
stubbornly dying

we are sinking in
petroleum fumes again
al

what is there to wake
to, the pit of our worry
at the end of days

WHAT IF HAIIKU

I have these spots now
on my lungs...what do they mean
are they canerous

i breathe slowly in
have slight shortness of my breath
it could be something

i dont know a thing
i dont know where we go now
at the end of life

SICK AUTUMN HAIKU

i am diseased now
full of shriveling coldness
at the noon of fall

at the noon of fall
i am falling in a pit
i am dying blind

SICK DIZZYNESS HAIKU

feeling to fall off
of the cliff of our nature
to a vast abyss

nothing left to do
except excuse our pathways
off a warming cliff

then the world turns cold
then the air is gone from us
and we choke on ice

eyes turn toward the sun
vacant eyes look off a ways
blindly stare at space

THE MUSIC OF HORROR HAIKU

the music of fear
trembles from my voice again
into the back yard

the swamp in the back

sucks sound from my throat again
in a fearfull way

it is beaufiful
though, this music from the swamp
this life in my gut

COLD WEEK HAIKU

frosty morning now
..a long day of wait and chill
shivering at the tv

moaning against cold
reclining in a long chair
inside the art room

i disappear now
waiting for you till i sleep
and fall off to night

FRIDGID WEEK HAIKU

this week felt colder
things dropped by twenty degrees
and shivered themselves

and i wandered off
in my mind numbly waiting
for things to catch up

until friiday came
the operation arrived
to diagnose me

COLD STEEL HAIKU

this concrete jungle
this monolith electric
failing fossil fuel

when the planet warms
migrations follow, disease
comes upon us too

endless disfunction
in broad scheme of things too
...silently we wait

POST BIOPSY HAIKU

afterwards waiting
for the results of the test
....it was easy then

i don't know...why not
hope for the best and listen
thanksgiveing comes now

FOREST KISS HAIKU

deep in the recess
if feel the kisses of trrees
we both love alot

i feel the same love
for nature that we bothe feel

now and forever

i feel the burning
cold in winter, hot later
in the year in time

FROST IN NOVEMBER HAIKU

there is already
frost on the ground in aumtumn
and snow further north

in spite of the earth
warming too much now, things have
gotten very cold

winter is here now
early in the season too
angel wings in snow

DECEMBER COMES HAIKU

the deep dark seeps in
the time of snow is here now
the spruce tree darkens

here in november
i wait for the other month
for the deeper month

and slowly she creeps
on legs like a leopard
she comes to stalk us

ONCE A WEEK HAIKU

the treatment follows
once a week, radiation
on the point of cancer

i don't know how tired
i'll be from the orocedure
five weeks and its gone

the earth may be dead
soon, unlike the earth i miissed
my fate for a while

THE LEAVES DANCE HAIKU

the leaves are browning
and in their brownness danceing
falling to their fate

the hour is quite late
or dark at least, though early
for the sun to peak

waiting for winter
and the naked hour to come
stripped trees dangling dumb

LOST HAIKU

leaves crrack under shoe
..the trip of the backyard swamp
toward journies thither

we trudge on aimless
without future hope, we do
until the end's pit

but what beauty now
what beautiful things we will see
these days of journey

WET WEATHER HAIKU

the rain came in pales,
buckets of water spilling
over our back yard

it went wet all day
paining our pores with dropets,
blurring our eyes up

i retreated to
the bedroom where i collapsed,
fell asleep and dreamed

WINTER SNAKES HAIKU

the cold reptillian
core of us sinks into mud
and falls fast asleep

december iinches
into time in a moment
where we lose ourselves

long before the ides
winter is assured to us
the trees are stripped bare

LOVER HAIKU

sweet strong woman joined
to my heart in a union
of a matriarchy

little girl who i love
and cuddle and hold closer
than my own heart now

love beyond tears too
beyond all hoping to sing
of our shared burden

DECEMBERING HAIKU

the mulch in the swamp
in the backyard looks stunning
when a deer goes by

i look through my perch
next to a window in here
and glow in the dark

soon daylight comes in
and shines on the porch out there
while is sit a watch

TRAILS TO NOWHERE

the beaufiul song
on the nowhere trails we take
echo their stanzas

again and again
in circles they follow on
singing their stazas

to nowhere in joy
to nowhere bautifully
onward and onward

DECEMBERS RAINS HAIKU

december rained much
buckets on the garden swamp
disappearing there

inside i sang songs
of sadness, dirges for us
to mumble thinking

sometimes i think cold
silly rainy thoughts for us
to sing about now

CANCERS DREAM OF SPREADING HAIKU

the boil on my chest
would turn to a pustulate
lava of virus

would turn to a spread
of cancerous magarine
in places i dread

my paranoid dread
is unstoppable boiling
from chest to extremes

THE COLD SWAMP HAIKU

the cold swamp kills me
it covers me with brambles
and numbs up my dread

soon in this woodlannd
there will come a winter storm
the snowflakes burry

there will be hereon
a wordless word of god come
to free us from want

SOLSTICE HAIKU

the black night of now
the frozen middle of it
when we stare ahead

my lover sleeps now
and i tremble to the sink
to taste of water

when i sleep i dream
of my cancer, and shiver
when i wake up too

TUMOR HAIKU

my cancer arrives
along with the dark cold air
outside in the back

christmas beckons us
the radiatiion tires me
i sleep long nighttimes

the season of joy
the season of dread as well
both things come to us

STRANGE DAYS HAIKU

strange days come to us
hot and cold and full of storm
blow upon our form

withered in winter
naked branches on a tree
light born of darkness

shivering at dawn
ghosts in terror finding us
shiveled on the floor

THE YULE HAIKU

christmas came frozen
dotting the back yard with ice
and brown twigs around

the christchild seemed dead
this strangest of years come here
frozen like a ghost

the gift of my love
she is all that sustains me
without her nothing

HAIKU KILLER CHILL

it came near christmas
arctic air that swept this place
snow and ice came tpo

not a pretty white snow
but weather north subzero
and here in the teens

and my depression
came as well dull headachey
staring out to dark

SORE CHEST HAIKU

first my ribs cracked up
airless i struggled minutes
then slept fulll of dope

out of hospitol
they sent my xray of chest
found a tumor there

start radiation
in five days of worrying
then doze the winter

WAITING HAIKU

i shiver in dark
waiting for you bright lovely
to come with warmth now

crawl under the quilt
and lie down in the darkness
wanting to hold you

all winter nighttime
your light is like christmas come
into my longing